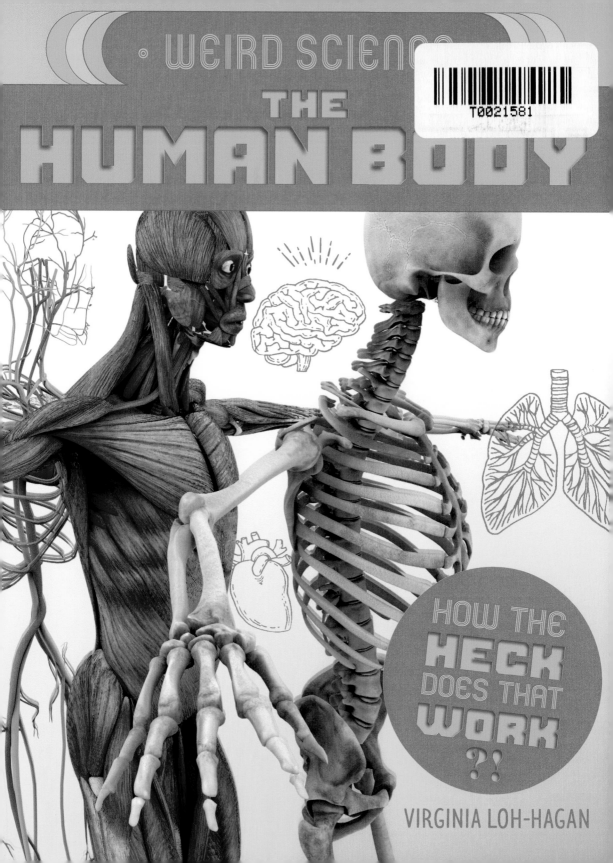

WEIRD SCIENCE

THE HUMAN BODY

HOW THE **HECK** DOES THAT **WORK** ?!

VIRGINIA LOH-HAGAN

45TH PARALLEL PRESS

Published in the United States of America by Cherry Lake Publishing Group
Ann Arbor, Michigan
www.cherrylakepublishing.com

Reading Adviser: Beth Walker Gambro, MS, Ed., Reading Consultant, Yorkville, IL
Book Designer: Felicia Macheske

Photo Credits: © © adike/Shutterstock, cover, back cover, 1; © Nadya Dobrynina/Shutterstock, cover, back cover, 1, 5; © Zheya/Shutterstock, back cover; © paulista/Shutterstock, back cover, 11; © Dmytro Vietrov/Shutterstock, 4; © Ljupco Smokovski/Shutterstock, 6; © Fer Gregory/Shutterstock, 7; © Mongkolchon Akesin/Shutterstock, 8; © Cryptographer/Shutterstock, 10; © Morakod1977/Shutterstock, 12; © Yurii Andreichyn/Shutterstock, 14; © fotoliza/Shutterstock, 15; © Diane Diederich/Shutterstock, 16; © Just dance/Shutterstock, 18; © Golden Shrimp/Shutterstock, 19; © Buntoon Rodseng/Shutterstock, 19; © khak/Shutterstock, 20; © Drawlab19/Shutterstock, 22; © KOHYAO/Shutterstock, 23; © Science Photo Library / Alamy Stock Photo, 24; © Fine Art Studio/Shutterstock, 26; © CkyBe/Shutterstock, 26; © Rocketclips, Inc./Shutterstock, 27; ©MDGRPHCS/Shutterstock, 28; © matias 216/Shutterstock, 30; © JRP Studio/Shutterstock, 31

45th Parallel Press is an imprint of Cherry Lake Publishing Group.

Library of Congress Cataloging-in-Publication Data

Names: Loh-Hagan, Virginia, author.
Title: Weird science : the human body / by Virginia Loh-Hagan.
Description: Ann Arbor, Michigan : Cherry Lake Publishing, 2021.
  | Series: How the heck does that work?! | Includes index.
Identifiers: LCCN 2021004900 (print) | LCCN 2021004901 (ebook)
  | ISBN 9781534187580 (hardcover) | ISBN 9781534188983 (paperback)
  | ISBN 9781534190382 (pdf) | ISBN 9781534191785 (ebook)
Subjects: LCSH: Human anatomy—Juvenile literature. | Human body—Juvenile
  literature. | Human physiology—Juvenile literature.
Classification: LCC QM27 .L64 2022 (print) | LCC QM27 (ebook) | DDC
  612—dc23
LC record available at https://lccn.loc.gov/2021004900
LC ebook record available at https://lccn.loc.gov/2021004901

Cherry Lake Publishing Group would like to acknowledge the work of the Partnership for 21st Century Learning, a Network of Battelle for Kids. Please visit *http://www.battelleforkids.org/networks/p21* for more information.

Printed in the United States of America
Corporate Graphics

Dr. Virginia Loh-Hagan is an author, university professor, and former classroom teacher. She's currently the Director of the Asian Pacific Islander Desi American Resource Center at San Diego State University. She's amazed by all the things the human body can do! She lives in San Diego with her very tall husband and very naughty dogs.

TABLE OF CONTENTS

INTRODUCTION 5

CHAPTER 1
BLOOD CIRCULATION 9

CHAPTER 2
GROWING BONES 13

CHAPTER 3
FARTS 17

CHAPTER 4
EARWAX 21

CHAPTER 5
REGENERATION 25

CHAPTER 6
USELESS BODY PARTS 29

GLOSSARY 32

LEARN MORE 32

INDEX 32

Water makes up about 50 to 60 percent of our bodies.
Babies and children have the highest percentage of water.

INTRODUCTION

All kinds of weird science happen in our bodies. Being alive takes a lot of work. Our bodies are working all the time. They do things without our thinking about it. They're amazing machines of nature.

Anatomy is the study of body parts. Human bodies have many parts. The basic parts are the head, neck, chest area, arms, and legs. Bodies are held together by bones and muscles. Bones and muscles allow us to move.

Human bodies have many organs. Organs are groups of tissues. Tissues are the materials that form parts of your body. Organs have specific jobs. The skin is our largest organ. It protects our bodies. It keeps out germs. It keeps our bodies cool or warm.

Other important organs are the brain, heart, kidney, liver, and lungs. The human brain controls our bodies. It receives and sends signals to other body organs. The heart pumps blood throughout our bodies. Kidneys remove waste. The liver cleans blood. Lungs help us breathe.

Organs are part of a system. Our bodies have several systems. These systems have specific jobs. One system moves blood. One moves air. Another system breaks down and takes in food. Still another system fights sicknesses. Another system breaks food down. It removes human waste. This waste is poop and pee.

Dare to learn more about the human body! So much is going on. How the heck does it all work?

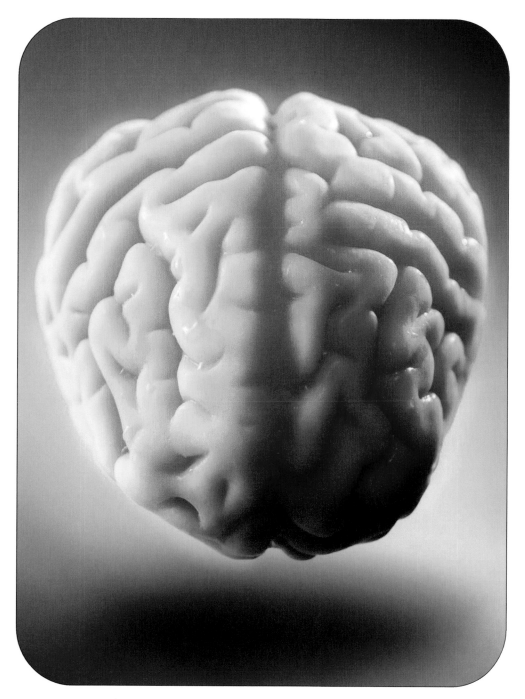

Human brains are made of 60 percent fat. They weigh about 3 pounds (1.4 kilograms).

Newborn babies have the fastest heartbeats.

CHAPTER 1

BLOOD CIRCULATION

Did you know our bodies are made up of highways? These highways carry blood. Cars need oil and gas to run. Our bodies need blood.

Blood is part of the **circulatory** system. Circulate means to travel. Blood circulates throughout the body. It keeps us alive. It brings nutrients and oxygen to all body parts. It carries waste to organs that get rid of it. It fights off sicknesses. It keeps our bodies cool and warm as needed.

Circulation starts at the heart. The heart is a pump. It beats about 60 to 100 times per minute. Each heartbeat pumps out blood to the lungs. It picks up oxygen-rich blood. This blood sends out oxygen. It returns to the heart. The heart pumps out blood to the lungs again. It picks up more oxygen. This cycle repeats.

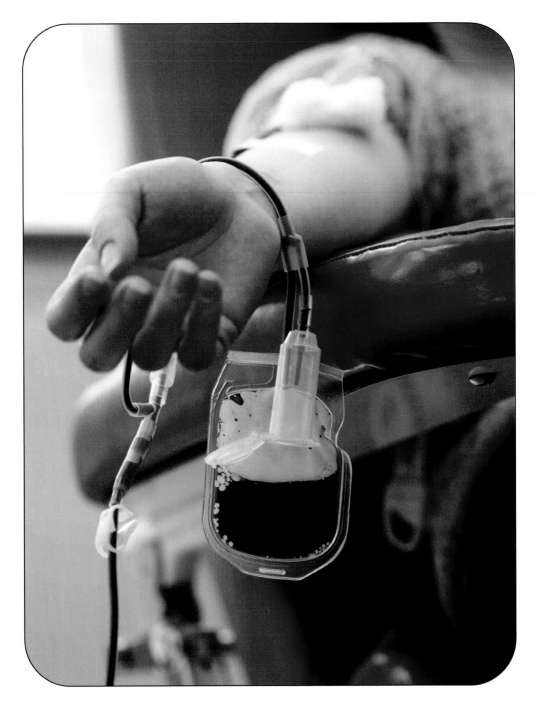

Adults have about 10 to 12 pints (4.7 to 5.7 liters)
of blood flowing through their bodies.

Blood travels in hollow tubes called blood **vessels**. They carry blood away from and back to the heart. **Arteries** and **veins** are types of blood vessels. Arteries carry blood away from the heart. They deliver nutrients and oxygen. Veins carry blood back to the heart. Blood in veins doesn't have much oxygen.

Each body part has a network of **capillaries**. Capillaries play an important role in sending oxygen in the blood to tissues. Capillaries are tiny blood vessels. They lead to small veins. Small veins lead to larger veins as blood nears the heart.

This system of vessels is a complicated highway. When put together, it's very long. It's more than 60,000 miles (96,561 kilometers) long. A person's blood vessels could wrap around the planet about 2.5 times.

Some kids and teens feel growing pains.
They especially feel it in their legs.

CHAPTER 2

GROWING BONES

Have you ever wondered how people grow taller? Human bones grow. They support our bodies. They help form our shapes. They're strong enough to support our weight. They protect our organs.

Bones have **collagen**. Collagen is connective tissue. It holds the body together. It keeps bones flexible. Bones also have calcium. Calcium keeps bones strong.

Newborn babies have about 300 tiny bones. Adults have 206 bones. As you grow, the tiny bones join together. They form bigger, longer bones. Bones are living tissues. These tissues are always renewing our bones. This renewal process slows down as we get older. There are 2 main processes.

Even WEIRDER BODY SCIENCE!

- Nose snot is mucus. Mucus is like human slime. Snot is good for us. It keeps noses from drying out. It traps germs and dust. It fights off sicknesses. Our bodies make about 2 pints (0.9 L) of mucus each day. Nose hairs sweep snot to the back of the throat. We swallow most of it. Some comes out of the nose. This often happens when people have colds. Boogers are dried snot in the nose.

- Saliva is often called spit. Spit is 99 percent water. Our bodies make about 2 to 6 cups (0.5 to 1.4 L) of spit a day. Spit lets us chew, swallow, and digest. Digest means to eat. It fights off germs. It keeps our teeth healthy. It washes away bits of food. It also helps us taste things.

- Long ago, big toes helped early humans grab things. Humans used their toes to climb trees or hang onto their mothers. Today, our big toes are mainly used to carry weight as we walk. They can also be used for toe-to-thumb transfers. Some people lose their thumbs in accidents. Surgeons cut off big toes. They replace the lost thumbs with big toes. This helps people grip things again.

First, bones build new bone cells. Bones are made of a network of calcium cells. Young bones have **cartilage** cells. Cartilage is a connective tissue. It's like rubber. These cells are at the end of bones. They multiply. They add new calcium to the bones. This makes bones grow longer and stronger. Kids have layers of these cells. These cell layers are called growth plates. These plates grow. Then, they change into hard bone. They close when kids reach their full adult heights.

Second, bones remove old bone cells. Once bones become hard, cartilage cells die. They form tiny pockets in bones. Blood vessels grow into these pockets. They drop in cells that add more calcium.

Most girls mature faster than boys. This means their growth plates change into hard bones faster.

Different gases mix in our stomach.
They make farts smell bad.

CHAPTER 3

FARTS

Did you know most people fart around 14 to 22 times a day? Everybody farts. Farting is a natural part of life.

Farts are part of the **digestion** process. It means to break down foods. Your body needs food. Your body processes the food you eat. Bodies make food usable for energy and survival. They take in what they need. They get rid of what they don't need. That comes out as poop, pee, and farts.

When you eat, you swallow food. But you also swallow air. This air has gases. Small bits of these gases travel through your body. The gases build up. They have to escape somehow.

OOPS...

Your body can **absorb** some of the gases. Absorb means to take in. Sometimes, too much gas builds up. Gases gather in the upper part of the **colon**. The colon is a large tube. It's also called the large intestine. Its job is to turn processed liquid waste into firm poop. It helps pass poop from our bodies.

The built-up gases put pressure on the colon wall. This can cause stomach pain. Sometimes, it causes pain in the chest. Your body wants to relieve the pain. So, your body pushes the pressure out as farts or burps. Farts come out of your butt. Burps come out of your mouth.

There are clothes designed to trap in bad fart smells.

UNSOLVED MYSTERY

Everybody yawns. Babies yawn. Animals yawn. When we yawn, our mouths open. Our jaws stretch. This increases the blood flow. We breathe in deeply. We take in air. This brings in more oxygen into the blood. It moves carbon dioxide out of the blood. Carbon dioxide is naturally produced when people breathe in and out. No one knows why we yawn. Early scientists thought yawning was about sucking in good air while pushing out bad air. Some scientists think yawning helps cool our brains. Brain temperatures rise when we're tired, bored, or sick. Yawning may keep our brains from overheating. Other scientists think yawning stretches our lungs. Yawning may help flex muscles and joints. It may increase heart rates. It may make us feel more awake. One thing about yawning is for sure. Yawning is catchy. People yawn when they see others yawn. They yawn when thinking about yawning. You may have yawned just now reading about yawning! (Did you?) This makes scientists think yawning is about sending messages. Yawning may be communicating how the body feels.

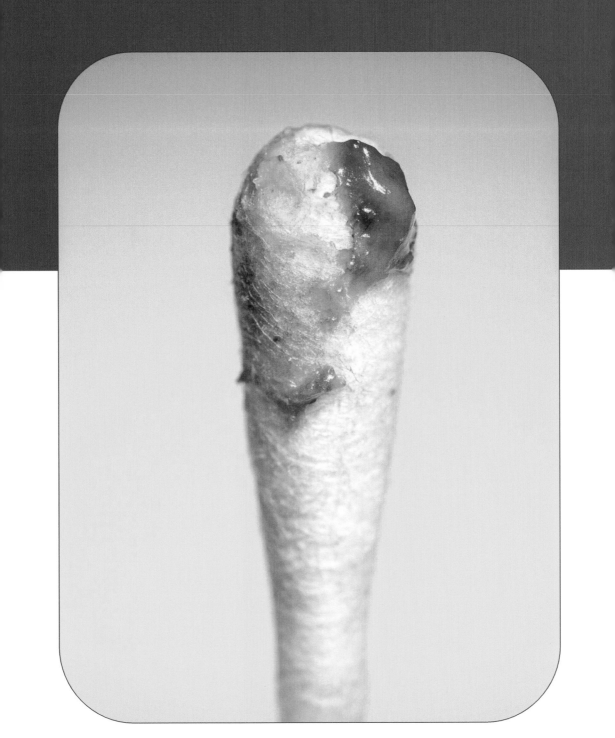

The scientific name for earwax is cerumen.

CHAPTER 4

EARWAX

Have you ever stuck a finger in your ear? You may feel something sticky. This is earwax. Earwax is a waxy oil. It's made of oil, sweat, dead skin cells, hair, and dirt. Earwax protects ears. It shields the eardrum. It keeps out dust and bugs. It keeps ears from drying out and itching. It fights off germs.

Ears are made of the ear **canal**, the middle ear, and the inner ear. Canals are passageways. Earwax is made in the ear canal. The canal is in the outer part of the ear. It's the area between the fleshy part of the ear and the middle ear. It's the passageway to the eardrum.

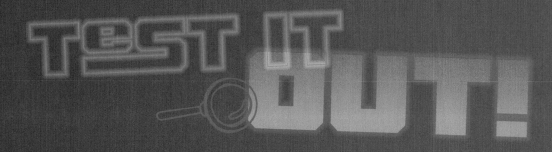

TEST IT OUT!

Intestines are long tubes. They're hollow. They run from our stomachs to our butts. We have a small intestine and a large intestine. The small intestine is about 20 to 25 feet (6.1 to 7.6 meters) long. It's 1 inch (2.5 centimeters) wide. It breaks down the food we eat. It takes in nutrients and water. It moves what's left into the large intestine. Learn more about the small intestine.

Materials

- Old garden hose or yarn
- Scissors or other cutting tool

1. Go outside. Stretch out the hose or yarn.

2. Measure it to 20 feet (6.1 m) and cut it off. This is how long your small intestine is!

3. Pick up the hose or yarn. Fold and scrunch it into a ball shape.

4. Try to fit it in front of your stomach. Try different shapes.

5. Think about how the small intestine is packed in your stomach area. Your intestine is more flexible than a garden hose. It's thicker than yarn. Your intestine can fit into a small space.

The ear canal has skin with **glands**. Glands are organs that secrete, or make, substances. The ear glands make earwax all the time. The canal always has enough wax in it.

After it's made, earwax moves through the ear canal. This is how ears clean themselves. Chewing and talking moves our lower jaws. This motion moves earwax around. Old earwax moves away from the eardrum. It moves toward the opening of the ear. It builds up. Then, it dries up and falls out. Or it flakes off or is removed when you wash. Washing your hair also washes your ears!

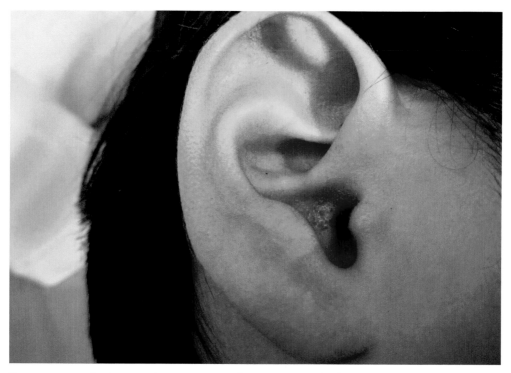

Some people have dry earwax. Some people have wetter earwax.

Humans lose about 50 million skin cells each day.
Skin cells live for about 4 weeks.

CHAPTER 5

REGENERATION

Have you ever had a sunburn? Sunburns damage the skin. But over a short period of time, the skin heals. This is how it happens. White blood cells move to the wound. Other cells also come to the rescue. These cells fill in the empty space left by the damaged skin. Healthy skin replaces the damaged skin. New hair, oil, and sweat glands form. Your skin **regenerates**. It regrows. But it's not like the original skin. It's different. It may have scars.

Our livers can regenerate. If part of the liver is lost, it can grow back. It can grow to its original size. But it doesn't grow to its original shape.

SCIENTIST SPOTLIGHT

Akrit Jaswal was born in India in 1993. He started studying the human body at age 5. He's the world's youngest surgeon. Surgeons are doctors who perform operations. Surgeons also treat sicknesses. Jaswal started walking and talking at 10 months old. He was reading and writing by age 2. At age 7, he performed his first surgery. Jaswal operated on an 8-year-old girl. The girl was burned in a fire. Her fingers had melted together. Jaswal freed her fingers. This surgery took an hour. Jaswal's parents filmed the surgery. They posted it online. The video became viral. Jaswal was called a "boy wonder." He's been on TV shows. At age 12, Jaswal started studying science at college. He's the youngest student to be accepted into a university in India. He learns from other surgeons. He visits hospitals. He wants to cure cancer. He studies how human bodies work.

Regeneration happens when our organs fix themselves after being damaged. Human bodies have the power to heal themselves. They respond to injury and sickness. Organs use remaining cells to heal. But there are limitations to regeneration. Deep injuries are hard to fix. Injuries can get infected. Infections slow down the healing process.

Humans can regenerate fingertips if the cells under the fingernails are still there. Humans can also regenerate bones if they're joined together. But humans can't grow back limbs. Limbs are legs or arms. This growth requires more than just replacing cells and tissues. For limbs, we need bones, muscles, blood vessels, and nerves. Our bodies can't grow what is gone.

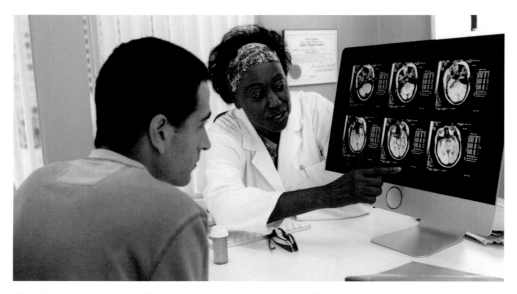

The human brain does not regenerate well.
It's hard to make new brain cells.

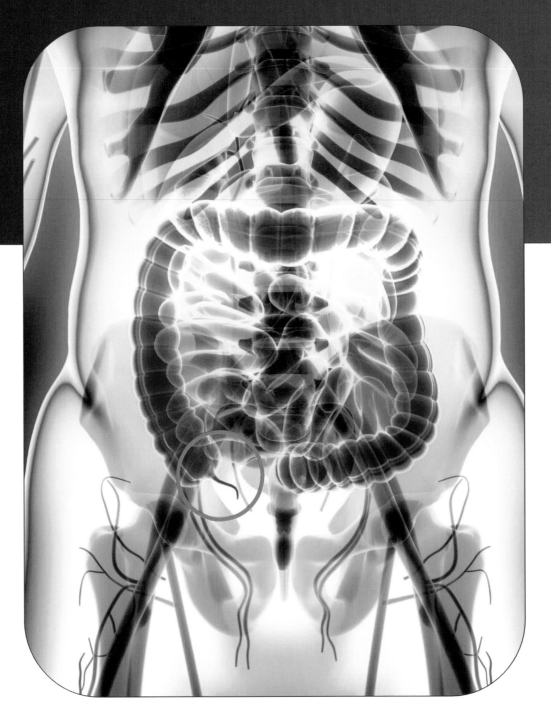

Ancient Egyptians called the appendix a "worm."

CHAPTER 6

USELESS BODY PARTS

Did you know your body doesn't use all of its parts? Most of your body parts have a specific job. But a few body parts don't have any job. These body parts were important for early humans. But they are no longer needed today. They can be removed. They don't affect people's lives at all.

The most well-known useless organ is the **appendix**. The appendix is a narrow pouch. It projects from the colon. It helped early humans digest tough plants. Today, we eat more meat. We have a more diverse diet. We don't need the appendix.

Early humans lived more than 2 million years ago.

Wisdom teeth also serve no purpose today. Early humans needed these extra back teeth. They needed them to tear and grind meat and raw grains. Today, we eat more soft foods. We eat more cooked grains. Also, over time, our brains grew bigger. Our jaws got smaller. This reduced space in the mouth. This crowded out wisdom teeth. Today, most people have them removed.

Your body has muscle fibers. These fibers make your hair stand on its end. Early humans were hairy. The fibers alerted them to fear or the cold. They made their body hair stick out. This made them look bigger. It made them look scarier. Today, they give you goose bumps.

GLOSSARY

absorb (ab-ZORB) to take in

anatomy (uh-NAT-uh-mee) the study of body parts

appendix (uh-PEN-diks) a narrow pouch projecting from the colon

arteries (AR-tuh-rees) blood vessels that carry oxygen-rich blood away from the heart to other parts of the body

canal (kuh-NAL) a passageway

capillaries (KAP-uh-ler-ees) tiny blood vessels that lead to veins

cartilage (KAR-tuh-lij) flexible connective tissue

circulatory (SUHR-kyuh-luh-tor-ee) relating to the circulation system

collagen (KAH-luh-juhn) connective tissue that holds the body together

colon (KOH-luhn) the large intestine whose job is to process and pass poop

digestion (duh-JESS-chuhn) the process of breaking down foods in the body

glands (GLANDS) special organs that make secretions

regenerates (ri-JEH-nuh-rayts) regrows

veins (VAYNS) blood vessels that carry blood back to the heart

vessels (VESS-uhls) hollow tubes used to transport blood

LEARN MORE

Bennett, Howard. *The Fantastic Body: What Makes You Tick & How You Get Sick.* Emmaus, PA: Rodale Kids, 2017.

Brosnan, Katie. *Gut Garden: A Journey Into the Wonderful World of Your Microbiome.* London, UK: Cicada Books, 2020.

Wilsdon, Christina, Patricia Daniels, and Jen Agrestra. *Ultimate Body-pedia: An Amazing Inside-Out Tour of the Human Body.* Washington, DC: National Geographic Kids, 2014.

INDEX

air, 6
anatomy, 5
appendix, 28, 29
arteries, 11

blood, 6, 10, 19
    circulation, 8–11
body parts, useless, 28–31
bones, 5, 12–15, 27
brain, 6, 7, 19, 27, 31
burps, 18

calcium, 13, 15
capillaries, 11
cartilage, 15
cells, 15, 27
    skin, 24, 25
cerumen, 20–23
circulation, blood, 8–11
collagen, 13
colon, 18, 29

digestion, 17, 29

earwax, 20–23

farts, 16–18
fat, 7
fibers, muscle, 31
food, 6, 17, 22

gases, 16, 17, 18
germs, 5, 14, 21
glands, 23
goose bumps, 31
growing pains, 12
growth plates, 15

healing, 27
heart, 6, 9, 11
heartbeats, 8, 9
human body
    introduction, 4–7
    unsolved mystery, 19
    weird science, 14

infections, 27
intestines, 18, 22

Jaswal, Akrit, 26

kidney, 6

limbs, 27
liver, 6, 25
lungs, 6, 9, 19

movements, 6
mucus, 14

nose, 14
nutrients, 9, 11

organs, 5–6, 27
oxygen, 9, 11

pee, 6, 17
poop, 6, 17, 18

regeneration, 24–27

saliva, 14
scars, 25
sicknesses, 6
skin, 5, 23
    cells, 24, 25
snot, 14
spit, 14
stomach, 16, 22
surgery, 26

teeth, 14, 31
tissues, 5, 13
toes, 14

veins, 11
vessels, 11, 15

waste, human, 6, 9, 18
wisdom teeth, 31

yawning, 19